THE **TESTING** SERIES

FUEL CALCULATION TESTS

Orders: Please contact How2become Ltd, Suite 2, 50 Churchill Square Business Centre, Kings Hill, Kent ME19 4YU.

You can also order via the e mail address info@how2become.co.uk.

ISBN: 9781909229006

First published 2012

Typeset for How2become Ltd by Molly Hill, Canada.

Printed in Great Britain for How2become Ltd by Bell & Bain Ltd, 303 Burnfield Road, Thornliebank, Glasgow G46 7UQ.

DISCLAIMER AND COPYRIGHT NOTICE

ABOUT FUEL CALCULATIONS

This guide contains a large number of fuel calculation tests which are designed to help you prepare for your assessment; however, before I provide you with the tests it is important to provide you with some important information about the test and also a number of sample test questions and explanations.

Fuel calculation questions are used in everyday life, from calculating how much gas you use in your own home to calculating the fuel required to launch a space shuttle into space. It is important that the people whose job it is to carry out these calculations do them confidently and correctly as a mistake could mean that an aircraft may not reach its destination because it does not have enough fuel remaining, for example.

You are reading this now because you need to practice how to solve fuel calculation questions. The reality is that there are procedures and methods to solving these types of questions.

It is worth remembering the following golden rules:

1. Always make sure that when doing a calculation you are using the correct units. For example, the formula for calculating time is:

Time = distance ÷ speed

Let's say that the distance travelled is given in miles. The speed will then need to be in miles per hour or miles per second or miles per minute. The speed cannot be in metres per hour or metres per second or metres per minute or centimetres per minute, simply because distance was initially given in miles. The units always need to consistent.

2. You should know that 1 hour = 60 minutes. Do not forget how to convert hours into minutes and vice versa i.e. if you have 5 hours you want to convert into minutes, do not divide by 60 as shown: $5 \div 60 = 0.0833333$ *minutes* because 5 hours does not equal less than 1 whole minute! The correct calculation should be: $60 \times 5 = 300$ *minutes*

3. When you have a final answer for the amount of fuel required, just stop and think about your answer for a while. Ask yourself if it really makes sense. For example, if 60 kilograms of fuel is burnt in 1 minute and the question is asking for the fuel burnt after 3 minutes – your answer should be 180 kilograms. Your thoughts should be in the form: "If 60 kilograms are used up in 1 minute, 2 minutes will burn up double this amount and 3 minutes will use up 3 times 60 kilograms".

These tips will no doubt help you with the questions provided on the following pages. If you are really struggling, detailed answers are provided below every question to assist you.

Confidence comes from practice and after going through the following questions, you will be able to do fuel calculations confidently.

SAMPLE QUESTIONS AND ANSWERS

QUESTION 1

You burn 36 kgs of fuel per hour. How much do you burn in 15 mins?

ANSWER TO QUESTION 1

36 kgs of fuel is burnt in one hour and one hour is equivalent to 60 minutes.

Method 1

15 minutes is a quarter of an hour (¼). Therefore, if ¼ is multiplied with 36kgs you will find how much is burnt in 15 minutes.

Amount of fuel burnt in 15 minutes = ***¼ × 36 kgs = 9 kgs***

Method 2 – Using cross multiplication

Step 1: Write out two columns as shown below and add the information given from the question (use x kilograms to represent 15 minutes worth of burnt fuel as we do not know how many kilograms are burnt in 15 minutes yet). The quantity x is what we need to calculate.

Kilograms	Time taken to burn
36 kgs	60 minutes
x kgs	15 minutes

Step 2: Cross multiply

Kilograms	Time taken to burn
36 kgs	60 minutes
x kgs	15 minutes

$$36 \times 15 = 60 \times x$$

Now isolate x by bringing the 60 across the other side of the equals sign:

$$\frac{36 \times 15}{60} = x$$

$$x = 9\ kgs$$

THE ANSWER TO QUESTION 1 IS 9 KGS

QUESTION 2

You burn 12 kgs of fuel per hour. How much fuel will you need to travel 44 miles if you average a speed of 66 mph?

ANSWER TO QUESTION 2

Using the formula: *time = distance ÷ speed*, the time taken to travel 44 miles can be calculated. This can then be used to calculate how much fuel was burnt for the 44 mile journey.

$$\text{time} = \text{distance} \div \text{speed}$$

$$= 44 \text{ miles} \div 66 \text{ mph}$$

$$= 0.66666667 \text{ hours}$$

To convert hours into minutes, multiply the hours by 60:

$$0.66666667 \text{ hours} = 0.66666667 \times 60 = 40 \text{ minutes}$$

Given that 12 kgs of fuel is burnt in 1 hour (60 minutes) we now need to work out how much fuel is burnt in 40 minutes.

40 minutes is: $\frac{40}{60} = \frac{2}{3}$ of an hour

If 12 kgs is now multiplied by ⅔, this will give the amount of fuel that was burnt for the 44 mile journey.

Amount of fuel burnt for the 44 mile journey = 12 × ⅔ = 8 *kgs*

THE ANSWER TO QUESTION 2 IS 8 KGS

QUESTION 3

You have used 50 kgs of fuel in the past 1 hour and 40 mins. How much do you burn per hour?

ANSWER TO QUESTION 3

1 hour and 40 mins is equal to 100 minutes.

50 kgs of fuel are burnt in 100 minutes and the question is asking how much is burnt every 60 minutes.

This can be solved using cross multiplication; the amount of fuel burnt every 60 minutes is labelled as 'x' for now:

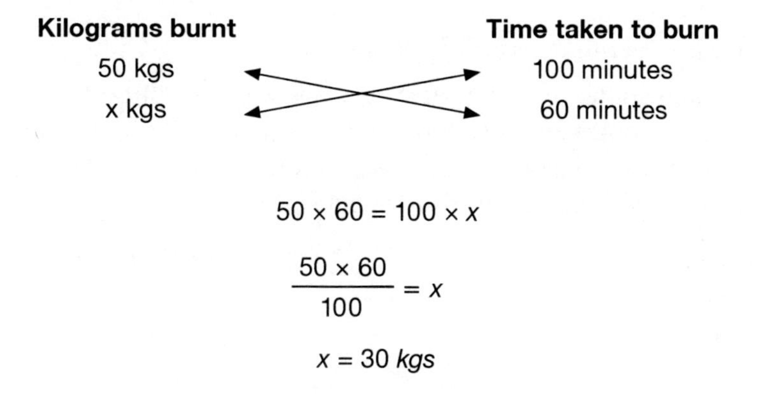

THE ANSWER TO QUESTION 3 IS 30 KGS

QUESTION 4

You burn 12 kgs of fuel per hour. How much do you burn in 40 mins?

ANSWER TO QUESTION 4

12 kgs of fuel are burnt in one hour and one hour is equivalent to 60 minutes.

Method 1

40 minutes is equivalent to two thirds of an hour (2/3). Therefore, if 2/3 is multiplied with 12kgs you will find how much is burnt in 40 minutes.

Amount of fuel burnt in 40 minutes= $2/3 \times 12$ kgs=8 kgs

Method 2 – Using cross multiplication

Step 1: Write out two columns as shown below and add the information given from the question (use x kilograms to represent 15 minutes worth of burnt fuel as we do not know how many kilograms are burnt in 15 minutes yet). The quantity x is what we need to calculate.

Kilograms	**Time taken to burn**
12 kgs	60 minutes
x kgs	40 minutes

Step 2: Cross multiply

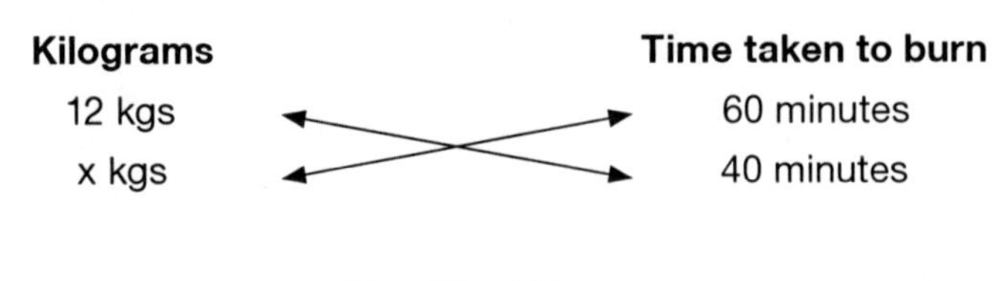

$$12 \times 40 = 60 \times x$$

Now isolate x by bringing the 60 across the other side of the equals sign:

$$\frac{12 \times 40}{60} = x$$

$$x = 8\ kgs$$

THE ANSWER TO QUESTION 4 IS 8 KGS

QUESTION 5

You burn 6 kgs of fuel per minute. How much do you burn in 1 hour and 10 mins?

ANSWER TO QUESTION 5

1 minute is equal to 6 kgs of fuel being burnt. Multiply this by 60 and this gives the amount of fuel burnt in 60 minutes (1 hour).

$$6\ kgs \times 60 = 360\ kgs$$

Therefore, in 60 minutes (1 hour) 360 kgs of fuel is burnt.

1 minute is equal to 6 kgs of fuel being burnt, so if 6 kg is multiplied by 10, this will give the amount of fuel burnt in 10 minutes:

$$6\ kgs \times 10 = 60\ kgs$$

Now add the amount of fuel burnt in 60 minutes (1 hour) to the amount of fuel burnt in 10 minutes to give the total amount burnt in 1 hour and 10 mins:

$$360\ kgs + 60\ kgs = 420\ kgs$$

THE ANSWER TO QUESTION 4 IS 420 KGS

QUESTION 6

You travel 408 miles. How much fuel will you need if you burn 30 kgs per hour, and are travelling at 255 mph?

ANSWER TO QUESTION 6

Using the formula: *time = distance ÷ speed*, the time taken to travel 408 miles can be calculated. This can then be used to calculate how much fuel was burnt for the 408 mile journey.

$$time = distance \div speed$$

$$= 408\ miles \div 255\ mph$$

$$= 1.6\ hours$$

To convert hours into minutes, multiply 1.6 hours by 60:

$$1.6\ hours = 1.6 \times 60 = 96\ minutes$$

Given that 30 kgs of fuel is burnt in 1 hour (60 minutes) we now need to work out how much fuel is burnt in 96 minutes.

This can be solved using cross multiplication where 'x' kgs is the amount of fuel burnt in 96 minutes:

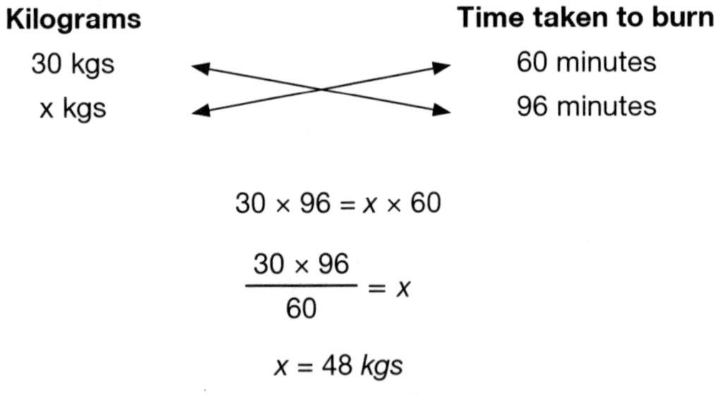

$$30 \times 96 = x \times 60$$

$$\frac{30 \times 96}{60} = x$$

$$x = 48\ kgs$$

Amount of fuel burnt for the 408 mile journey = 48 kgs

THE ANSWER TO QUESTION 6 IS 48 KGS

QUESTION 7

You travel 68 miles. How much fuel will you need if you burn 2 kgs per hour, and are travelling at 68 mph?

ANSWER TO QUESTION 7

Using the formula: time=distance÷speed, the time taken to travel 68 miles can be calculated. This can then be used to calculate how much fuel was burnt for the 68 mile journey.

$$time = distance \div speed$$
$$= 68\ miles \div 68\ mph$$
$$= 1\ hour$$

Given that 2 kgs of fuel is burnt in 1 hour this means that because it took 1 hour to travel 68 miles, 2 kgs of fuel only were burnt.

Amount of fuel burnt for the 68 *mile journey* = 2 *kgs*

THE ANSWER TO QUESTION 7 IS 2 KGS

QUESTION 8

You have used 12 kgs of fuel in the past 48 mins. How much do you burn per hour?

ANSWER TO QUESTION 8

Using cross multiplication, label 'x' as the amount of fuel burnt per hour (60 minutes)

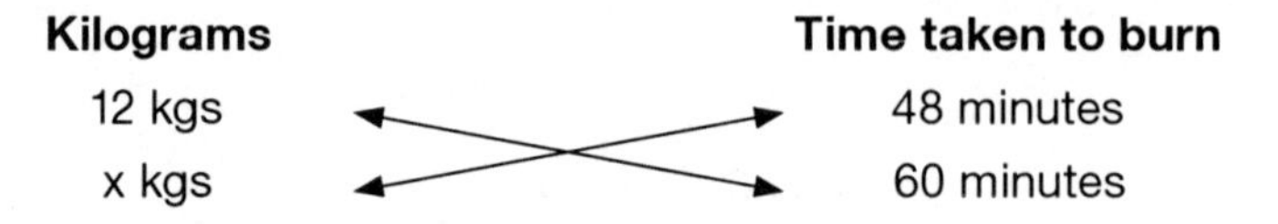

The calculation becomes:

$$12 \times 60 = x \times 48$$

$$\frac{12 \times 60}{48} = x$$

$$x = 15\ kgs$$

Amount of fuel burnt per hour = 15 *kgs*

THE ANSWER TO QUESTION 8 IS 15 KGS

QUESTION 9

You travel 176 miles. How much fuel will you need if you burn 60 kgs per hour, and are travelling at 440 mph?

ANSWER TO QUESTION 9

Using the formula: *time = distance ÷ speed*, the time taken to travel 176 miles can be calculated. This can then be used to calculate how much fuel was required for the 176 mile journey.

$$time = distance \div speed$$

$$= 176\ miles \div 440\ mph$$

$$= 0.4\ hours$$

Given that 60 kgs of fuel is burnt in 1 hour (60 minutes) we now need to work out how much fuel is burnt in 0.4 hours.

This can be solved using cross multiplication where 'x' kgs is the amount of fuel burnt in 0.4 hours:

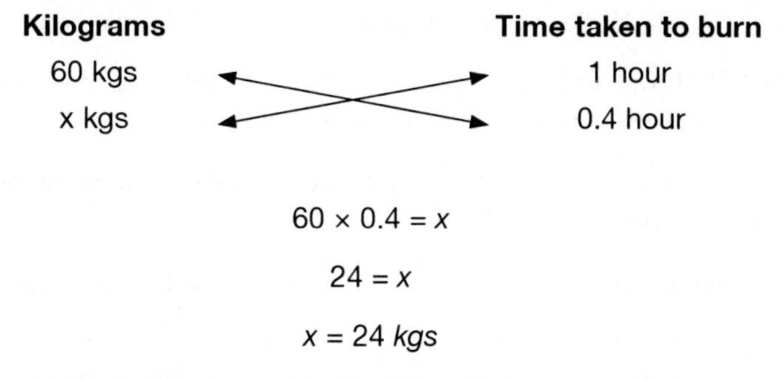

$$60 \times 0.4 = x$$

$$24 = x$$

$$x = 24\ kgs$$

Amount of fuel used for the 176 mile journey = 24 kgs

THE ANSWER TO QUESTION 9 IS 24 KGS

QUESTION 10

You travel 589 NM. How much fuel will you need if you burn 75 lbs per hour, and are travelling at 465 kts?

ANSWER TO QUESTION 10

Note: NM stands for nautical miles; it is another unit for distance used, for example on aircraft and ships. Also used on aircraft and ships to measure their speeds is the unit called 'knots' (kts).

Using the formula: *time = distance ÷ speed*, the time taken to travel 589 NM can be calculated. This can then be used to calculate how much fuel was burnt for the 589 NM mile journey.

$$time = distance \div speed$$

$$= 589\ NM \div 465\ knots$$

$$= 1.26666667\ hours$$

To convert hours into minutes, multiply 1.26666667 hours by 60:

$$1.26666667\ hours = 1.26666667 \times 60 = 76\ minutes$$

Given that 75 lbs of fuel is burnt in 1 hour (60 minutes) we now need to work out how much fuel, in lbs, is burnt in 76 minutes.

This can be solved using cross multiplication where 'x' lbs is the amount of fuel burnt in 76 minutes:

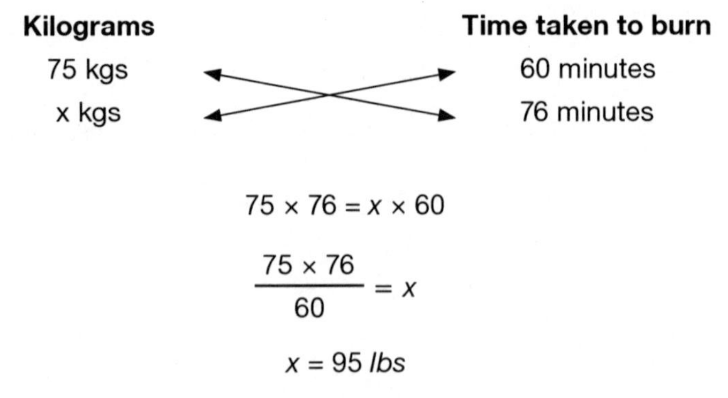

$$75 \times 76 = x \times 60$$

$$\frac{75 \times 76}{60} = x$$

$$x = 95\ lbs$$

Amount of fuel used for the 589 NM mile journey = 95 lbs

Well done for completing the questions on fuel calculations. The only way these questions will get harder in real life is if units are given in which you need to convert to a different unit – for example lbs into kgs, centimetres into metres etc.

The fact is, you have now learnt the method for tackling these types of problems and will therefore be able to tackle any similar questions thrown at you regardless of which units are used.

I have now provided you with 12 sample tests containing a total of 300 questions to help you prepare further. I have deliberately not provided a time limit to each test as I believe the most important aspect to your preparation is to answer the questions within each test correctly. The answers to each test are supplied following each test.

Please note: You will find that some of the questions that follow easy to answer and others more difficult. This has been done deliberately. I have found that many candidates who apply for technical posts either in the Armed Forces or the Airline Industry are just as likely to fall down on the easy questions, as they are the more difficult ones. You will also find that some of the question styles are repetitive. Again, I have done this deliberately. If you complete the workbook you will find that you become proficient and competent when it comes to tackling Fuel Calculation Tests. Good luck.

FUEL CALCULATION TESTS

FUEL CALCULATION TEST 1

QUESTION 1

You burn 90 kgs of fuel per hour. How much fuel will you need to travel 23 miles if you average a speed of 230 mph?

Answer:

QUESTION 2

You have used 24 kgs of fuel in the past 2 hours. How much do you burn per hour?

Answer:

QUESTION 3

You travel 72 NM. How much fuel will you need if you burn 270 kgs per hour, and are travelling at 720 kts?

Answer:

QUESTION 4

You travel 65 NM. How much fuel will you need if you burn 15 lbs per hour, and are travelling at 65 kts?

Answer:

QUESTION 5

You travel 18 miles. How much fuel will you need if you burn 16 kgs per minute, and are travelling at 36 mph?

Answer:

QUESTION 6

You have used 1 kg of fuel in the past 30 mins. How much do you burn per hour?

Answer:

QUESTION 7

You travel 9 miles. How much fuel will you need if you burn 18 kgs per hour, and are travelling at 18 mph?

Answer:

QUESTION 8

You burn 120 kgs of fuel per hour. How much do you burn in 12 mins?

Answer:

QUESTION 9

You travel 513 NM. How much fuel will you need if you burn 30 lbs per hour, and are travelling at 285 kts?

Answer:

QUESTION 10

You have used 215 kgs of fuel in the past 2 hours and 52 mins. How much do you burn per hour?

Answer:

QUESTION 11

You burn 32 kgs of fuel per hour. How much do you burn in 30 mins?

Answer:

QUESTION 12

You travel 8 NM. How much fuel will you need if you burn 30 kgs per minute, and are travelling at 20 kts?

Answer:

QUESTION 13

You burn 45 kgs of fuel per hour. How much do you burn in 24 mins?

Answer:

QUESTION 14

You burn 24 kgs of fuel per hour. How much fuel will you need to travel 77 miles if you average a speed of 84 mph?

Answer:

QUESTION 15

You burn 240 kgs of fuel per hour. How much fuel will you need to travel 153 miles if you average a speed of 270 mph?

Answer:

QUESTION 16

You burn 150 kgs of fuel per hour. How much do you burn in 22 mins?

Answer:

QUESTION 17

You burn 75 kgs of fuel per hour. How much do you burn in 20 mins?

Answer:

QUESTION 18

You have used 100 kgs of fuel in the past 2 hours and 30 mins. How much do you burn per hour?

Answer:

QUESTION 19

You burn 12 kgs of fuel per minute. How much do you burn in 30 mins?

Answer:

QUESTION 20

You travel 504 NM. How much fuel will you need if you burn 96 lbs per hour, and are travelling at 504 kts?

Answer:

QUESTION 21

You have used 21 kgs of fuel in the past 45 mins. How much do you burn per hour?

Answer:

QUESTION 22

You travel 572 NM. How much fuel will you need if you burn 105 kgs per minute, and are travelling at 660 kts?

Answer:

QUESTION 23

You travel at an average speed of 405 mph. How much fuel do you need for a 162 mile trip if you burn 150 kgs per hour?

Answer:

QUESTION 24

You burn 4 kgs of fuel per hour. How much fuel will you need to travel 38 miles if you average a speed of 76 mph?

Answer:

QUESTION 25

You burn 10 kgs of fuel per hour. How much do you burn in 48 mins?

Answer:

ANSWERS TO FUEL CALCULATION TEST 1

Question 1 – 9 kgs

Question 2 – 12 kgs

Question 3 – 27 kgs

Question 4 – 15 lbs

Question 5 – 480 kgs

Question 6 – 2 kgs

Question 7 – 9 kgs

Question 8 – 24 kgs

Question 9 – 54 lbs

Question 10 – 75 kgs

Question 11 – 16 kgs

Question 12 – 720 kgs

Question 13 – 18 kgs

Question 14 – 22 kgs

Question 15 – 136 kgs

Question 16 – 55 kgs

Question 17 – 25 kgs

Question 18 – 40 kgs

Question 19 – 360 kgs

Question 20 – 96 lbs

Question 21 – 28 kgs

Question 22 – 5460 kgs

Question 23 – 60 kgs

Question 24 – 2 kgs

Question 25 – 8 kgs

FUEL CALCULATION TEST 2

QUESTION 1

You travel 62 miles. How much fuel will you need if you burn 100 kgs per hour, and are travelling at 310 mph?

Answer:

QUESTION 2

You travel 168 NM. How much fuel will you need if you burn 12 lbs per hour, and are travelling at 112 kts?

Answer:

QUESTION 3

You travel 270 NM. How much fuel will you need if you burn 105 lbs per hour, and are travelling at 675 kts?

Answer:

QUESTION 4

You burn 40 kgs of fuel per minute. How much do you burn in 1 hour and 54 mins?

Answer:

QUESTION 5

You travel 6 miles. How much fuel will you need if you burn 4 kgs per hour, and are travelling at 4 mph?

Answer:

QUESTION 6

You burn 30 kgs of fuel per minute. How much do you burn in 1 hour and 20 mins?

Answer:

QUESTION 7

You burn 40 kgs of fuel per minute. How much do you burn in 1 hour and 36 mins?

Answer:

QUESTION 8

You travel 255 NM. How much fuel will you need if you burn 84 lbs per hour, and are travelling at 180 kts?

Answer:

QUESTION 9

You have used 460 kgs of fuel in the past 3 hours and 50 mins. How much do you burn per hour?

Answer:

QUESTION 10

You have used 12 kgs of fuel in the past 48 mins. How much do you burn per hour?

Answer:

QUESTION 11

You travel at an average speed of 690 mph. How much fuel do you need for a 322 mile trip if you burn 300 kgs per hour?

Answer:

QUESTION 12

You have used 250 kgs of fuel in the past 2 hours and 30 mins. How much do you burn per hour?

Answer:

QUESTION 13

You travel 60 NM. How much fuel will you need if you burn 4 lbs per hour, and are travelling at 60 kts?

Answer:

QUESTION 14

You burn 4 kgs of fuel per hour. How much do you burn in 15 mins?

Answer:

QUESTION 15

You have used 9 kgs of fuel in the past 20 mins. How much do you burn per hour?

Answer:

QUESTION 16

You travel 700 NM. How much fuel will you need if you burn 80 lbs per hour, and are travelling at 500 kts?

Answer:

QUESTION 17

You travel at an average speed of 900 mph. How much fuel do you need for a 810 mile trip if you burn 60 kgs per hour?

Answer:

QUESTION 18

You have used 28 kgs of fuel in the past 1 hour and 52 mins. How much do you burn per hour?

Answer:

QUESTION 19

You travel at an average speed of 960 mph. How much fuel do you need for a 256 mile trip if you burn 150 kgs per hour?

Answer:

QUESTION 20

You travel 132 NM. How much fuel will you need if you burn 160 kgs per minute, and are travelling at 440 kts?

Answer:

QUESTION 21

You burn 42 kgs of fuel per hour. How much do you burn in 30 mins?

Answer:

QUESTION 22

You travel 11 miles. How much fuel will you need if you burn 21 kgs per minute, and are travelling at 33 mph?

Answer:

QUESTION 23

You burn 3 kgs of fuel per hour. How much do you burn in 40 mins?

Answer:

QUESTION 24

You travel 91 miles. How much fuel will you need if you burn 50 kgs per hour, and are travelling at 130 mph?

Answer:

QUESTION 25

You burn 48 kgs of fuel per hour. How much do you burn in 20 mins?

Answer:

ANSWERS TO FUEL CALCULATION TEST 2

Question 1 – 20 kgs

Question 2 – 18 lbs

Question 3 – 42 lbs

Question 4 – 4560 kgs

Question 5 – 6 kgs

Question 6 – 2400 kgs

Question 7 – 3840 kgs

Question 8 – 119 lbs

Question 9 – 120 kgs

Question 10 – 15 kgs

Question 11 – 140 kgs

Question 12 – 100 kgs

Question 13 – 4 lbs

Question 14 – 1 kg

Question 15 – 27 kgs

Question 16 – 112 lbs

Question 17 – 54 kgs

Question 18 – 15 kgs

Question 19 – 40 kgs

Question 20 – 2880 kgs

Question 21 – 21 kgs

Question 22 – 420 kgs

Question 23 – 2 kgs

Question 24 – 35 kgs

Question 25 – 16 kgs

FUEL CALCULATION TEST 3

QUESTION 1

You burn 12 kgs of fuel per hour. How much do you burn in 20 mins?

Answer:

QUESTION 2

You travel 205 NM. How much fuel will you need if you burn 180 kgs per hour, and are travelling at 820 kts?

Answer:

QUESTION 3

You burn 8 kgs of fuel per hour. How much do you burn in 45 mins?

Answer:

QUESTION 4

You travel 32 miles. How much fuel will you need if you burn 120 kgs per hour, and are travelling at 96 mph?

Answer:

QUESTION 5

You travel at an average speed of 330 mph. How much fuel do you need for a 99 mile trip if you burn 80 kgs per hour?

Answer:

QUESTION 6

You travel 288 NM. How much fuel will you need if you burn 24 kgs per hour, and are travelling at 432 kts?

Answer:

QUESTION 7

You burn 100 kgs of fuel per hour. How much fuel will you need to travel 850 miles if you average a speed of 1000 mph?

Answer:

QUESTION 8

You travel 27 miles. How much fuel will you need if you burn 72 kgs per hour, and are travelling at 324 mph?

Answer:

QUESTION 9

You travel 28 NM. How much fuel will you need if you burn 90 kgs per hour, and are travelling at 210 kts?

Answer:

QUESTION 10

You have used 100 kgs of fuel in the past 3 hours and 20 mins. How much do you burn per hour?

Answer:

QUESTION 11

You travel 360 miles. How much fuel will you need if you burn 160 kgs per hour, and are travelling at 900 mph?

Answer:

QUESTION 12

You burn 3 kgs of fuel per hour. How much do you burn in 40 mins?

Answer:

QUESTION 13

You travel 40 miles. How much fuel will you need if you burn 6 kgs per hour, and are travelling at 80 mph?

Answer:

QUESTION 14

You travel at an average speed of 585 mph. How much fuel do you need for a 234 mile trip if you burn 90 kgs per hour?

Answer:

QUESTION 15

You travel at an average speed of 148 mph. How much fuel do you need for a 37 mile trip if you burn 16 kgs per hour?

Answer:

QUESTION 16

You burn 60 kgs of fuel per hour. How much fuel will you need to travel 38 miles if you average a speed of 228 mph?

Answer:

QUESTION 17

You travel 9 miles. How much fuel will you need if you burn 45 kgs per hour, and are travelling at 45 mph?

Answer:

QUESTION 18

You burn 48 kgs of fuel per minute. How much do you burn in 1 hour?

Answer:

QUESTION 19

You travel 48 NM. How much fuel will you need if you burn 24 lbs per hour, and are travelling at 48 kts?

Answer:

QUESTION 20

You have used 66 kgs of fuel in the past 2 hours and 12 mins. How much do you burn per hour?

Answer:

QUESTION 21

You burn 30 kgs of fuel per minute. How much do you burn in 1 hour and 48 mins?

Answer:

QUESTION 22

You burn 12 kgs of fuel per hour. How much fuel will you need to travel 36 miles if you average a speed of 432 mph?

Answer:

QUESTION 23

You burn 90 kgs of fuel per minute. How much do you burn in 1 hour and 4 mins?

Answer:

QUESTION 24

You burn 15 kgs of fuel per hour. How much fuel will you need to travel 20 miles if you average a speed of 60 mph?

Answer:

QUESTION 25

You have used 84 kgs of fuel in the past 2 hours and 48 mins. How much do you burn per hour?

Answer:

ANSWERS TO FUEL CALCULATION TEST 3

Question 1 – 4 kgs

Question 2 – 45 kgs

Question 3 – 6 kgs

Question 4 – 40 kgs

Question 5 – 24 kgs

Question 6 – 16 kgs

Question 7 – 85 kgs

Question 8 – 6 kgs

Question 9 – 12 kgs

Question 10 – 30 kgs

Question 11 – 64 kgs

Question 12 – 2 kgs

Question 13 – 3 kgs

Question 14 – 36 kgs

Question 15 – 4 kgs

Question 16 – 10 kgs

Question 17 – 9 kgs

Question 18 – 2880 kgs

Question 19 – 24 lbs

Question 20 – 30 kgs

Question 21 – 3240 kgs

Question 22 – 1 kg

Question 23 – 5760 kgs

Question 24 – 5 kgs

Question 25 – 30 kgs

FUEL CALCULATION TEST 4

QUESTION 1

You have used 416 kgs of fuel in the past 3 hours and 28 mins. How much do you burn per hour?

Answer:

QUESTION 2

You travel 9 NM. How much fuel will you need if you burn 6 kgs per minute, and are travelling at 27 kts?

Answer:

QUESTION 3

You burn 25 kgs of fuel per hour. How much do you burn in 36 mins?

Answer:

QUESTION 4

You burn 20 kgs of fuel per minute. How much do you burn in 1 hour and 3 mins?

Answer:

QUESTION 5

You travel 700 miles. How much fuel will you need if you burn 120 kgs per minute, and are travelling at 840 mph?

Answer:

QUESTION 6

You have used 776 kgs of fuel in the past 3 hours and 14 mins. How much do you burn per hour?

Answer:

QUESTION 7

You burn 15 kgs of fuel per hour. How much fuel will you need to travel 8 miles if you average a speed of 24 mph?

Answer:

QUESTION 8

You burn 30 kgs of fuel per hour. How much do you burn in 16 mins?

Answer:

QUESTION 9

You burn 135 kgs of fuel per hour. How much do you burn in 16 mins?

Answer:

QUESTION 10

You burn 9 kgs of fuel per hour. How much fuel will you need to travel 13 miles if you average a speed of 39 mph?

Answer:

QUESTION 11

You travel 138 NM. How much fuel will you need if you burn 30 kgs per hour, and are travelling at 230 kts?

Answer:

QUESTION 12

You burn 8 kgs of fuel per hour. How much do you burn in 30 mins?

Answer:

QUESTION 13

You have used 58 kgs of fuel in the past 2 hours and 25 mins. How much do you burn per hour?

Answer:

QUESTION 14

You burn 25 kgs of fuel per minute. How much do you burn in 12 mins?

Answer:

QUESTION 15

You burn 140 kgs of fuel per minute. How much do you burn in 33 mins?

Answer:

QUESTION 16

You burn 10 kgs of fuel per hour. How much do you burn in 12 mins?

Answer:

QUESTION 17

You travel 280 NM. How much fuel will you need if you burn 36 kgs per minute, and are travelling at 420 kts?

Answer:

QUESTION 18

You travel 26 miles. How much fuel will you need if you burn 24 kgs per hour, and are travelling at 312 mph?

Answer:

QUESTION 19

You travel 924 miles. How much fuel will you need if you burn 240 kgs per hour, and are travelling at 1320 mph?

Answer:

QUESTION 20

You burn 40 kgs of fuel per hour. How much do you burn in 42 mins?

Answer:

QUESTION 21

You have used 220 kgs of fuel in the past 1 hour and 28 mins. How much do you burn per hour?

Answer:

QUESTION 22

You burn 4 kgs of fuel per minute. How much do you burn in 1 hour and 30 mins?

Answer:

QUESTION 23

You burn 12 kgs of fuel per hour. How much do you burn in 30 mins?

Answer:

QUESTION 24

You travel 72 NM. How much fuel will you need if you burn 270 kgs per hour, and are travelling at 720 kts?

Answer:

QUESTION 25

You travel 65 NM. How much fuel will you need if you burn 15 lbs per hour, and are travelling at 65 kts?

Answer:

ANSWERS TO FUEL CALCULATION TEST 4

Question 1 – 120 kgs

Question 2 – 120 kgs

Question 3 – 15 kgs

Question 4 – 1260 kgs

Question 5 – 6000 kgs

Question 6 – 240 kgs

Question 7 – 5 kgs

Question 8 – 8 kgs

Question 9 – 36 kgs

Question 10 – 3 kgs

Question 11 – 18 kgs

Question 12 – 4 kgs

Question 13 – 24 kgs

Question 14 – 300 kgs

Question 15 – 4620 kgs

Question 16 – 2 kgs

Question 17 – 1440 kgs

Question 18 – 2 kgs

Question 19 – 168 kgs

Question 20 – 28 kgs

Question 21 – 150 kgs

Question 22 – 360 kgs

Question 23 – 6 kgs

Question 24 – 27 kgs

Question 25 – 15 lbs

FUEL CALCULATION TEST 5

QUESTION 1

You burn 240 kgs of fuel per hour. How much fuel will you need to travel 153 miles if you average a speed of 270 mph?

Answer:

QUESTION 2

You burn 150 kgs of fuel per hour. How much do you burn in 22 mins?

Answer:

QUESTION 3

You burn 75 kgs of fuel per hour. How much do you burn in 20 mins?

Answer:

QUESTION 4

You have used 100 kgs of fuel in the past 2 hours and 30 mins. How much do you burn per hour?

Answer:

QUESTION 5

You burn 12 kgs of fuel per minute. How much do you burn in 30 mins?

Answer:

QUESTION 6

You travel 504 NM. How much fuel will you need if you burn 96 lbs per hour, and are travelling at 504 kts?

Answer:

QUESTION 7

You have used 21 kgs of fuel in the past 45 mins. How much do you burn per hour?

Answer:

QUESTION 8

You travel 572 NM. How much fuel will you need if you burn 105 kgs per minute, and are travelling at 660 kts?

Answer:

QUESTION 9

You travel at an average speed of 405 mph. How much fuel do you need for a 162 mile trip if you burn 150 kgs per hour?

Answer:

QUESTION 10

You burn 4 kgs of fuel per hour. How much fuel will you need to travel 38 miles if you average a speed of 76 mph?

Answer:

QUESTION 11

You burn 10 kgs of fuel per hour. How much do you burn in 48 mins?

Answer:

QUESTION 12

You travel 62 miles. How much fuel will you need if you burn 100 kgs per hour, and are travelling at 310 mph?

Answer:

QUESTION 13

You travel 168 NM. How much fuel will you need if you burn 12 lbs per hour, and are travelling at 112 kts?

Answer:

QUESTION 14

You travel 270 NM. How much fuel will you need if you burn 105 lbs per hour, and are travelling at 675 kts?

Answer:

QUESTION 15

You burn 40 kgs of fuel per minute. How much do you burn in 1 hour and 54 mins?

Answer:

QUESTION 16

You travel 6 miles. How much fuel will you need if you burn 4 kgs per hour, and are travelling at 4 mph?

Answer:

QUESTION 17

You burn 30 kgs of fuel per minute. How much do you burn in 1 hour and 20 mins?

Answer:

QUESTION 18

You burn 40 kgs of fuel per minute. How much do you burn in 1 hour and 36 mins?

Answer:

QUESTION 19

You travel 255 NM. How much fuel will you need if you burn 84 lbs per hour, and are travelling at 180 kts?

Answer:

QUESTION 20

You have used 460 kgs of fuel in the past 3 hours and 50 mins. How much do you burn per hour?

Answer:

QUESTION 21

You travel 18 miles. How much fuel will you need if you burn 16 kgs per minute, and are travelling at 36 mph?

Answer:

QUESTION 22

You have used 1 kg of fuel in the past 30 mins. How much do you burn per hour?

Answer:

QUESTION 23

You travel 9 miles. How much fuel will you need if you burn 18 kgs per hour, and are travelling at 18 mph?

Answer:

QUESTION 24

You burn 120 kgs of fuel per hour. How much do you burn in 12 mins?

Answer:

QUESTION 25

You travel 513 NM. How much fuel will you need if you burn 30 lbs per hour, and are travelling at 285 kts?

Answer:

ANSWERS TO FUEL CALCULATION TEST 5

Question 1 – 136 kgs

Question 2 – 55 kgs

Question 3 – 25 kgs

Question 4 – 40 kgs

Question 5 – 360 kgs

Question 6 – 96 lbs

Question 7 – 28 kgs

Question 8 – 5460 kgs

Question 9 – 60 kgs

Question 10 – 2 kgs

Question 11 – 8 kgs

Question 12 – 20 kgs

Question 13 – 18 lbs

Question 14 – 42 lbs

Question 15 – 4560 kgs

Question 16 – 6 kgs

Question 17 – 2400 kgs

Question 18 – 3840 kgs

Question 19 – 119 lbs

Question 20 – 120 kgs

Question 21 – 480 kgs

Question 22 – 2 kgs

Question 23 – 9 kgs

Question 24 – 24 kgs

Question 25 – 54 lbs

FUEL CALCULATION TEST 6

QUESTION 1

You burn 90 kgs of fuel per hour. How much fuel will you need to travel 23 miles if you average a speed of 230 mph?

Answer:

QUESTION 2

You have used 24 kgs of fuel in the past 2 hours. How much do you burn per hour?

Answer:

QUESTION 3

You have used 215 kgs of fuel in the past 2 hours and 52 mins. How much do you burn per hour?

Answer:

QUESTION 4

You burn 32 kgs of fuel per hour. How much do you burn in 30 mins?

Answer:

QUESTION 5

You travel 8 NM. How much fuel will you need if you burn 30 kgs per minute, and are travelling at 20 kts?

Answer:

QUESTION 6

You burn 45 kgs of fuel per hour. How much do you burn in 24 mins?

Answer:

QUESTION 7

You burn 24 kgs of fuel per hour. How much fuel will you need to travel 77 miles if you average a speed of 84 mph?

Answer:

QUESTION 8

You have used 12 kgs of fuel in the past 48 mins. How much do you burn per hour?

Answer:

QUESTION 9

You travel at an average speed of 690 mph. How much fuel do you need for a 322 mile trip if you burn 300 kgs per hour?

Answer:

QUESTION 10

You have used 250 kgs of fuel in the past 2 hours and 30 mins. How much do you burn per hour?

Answer:

QUESTION 11

You travel 60 NM. How much fuel will you need if you burn 4 lbs per hour, and are travelling at 60 kts?

Answer:

QUESTION 12

You burn 4 kgs of fuel per hour. How much do you burn in 15 mins?

Answer:

QUESTION 13

You have used 9 kgs of fuel in the past 20 mins. How much do you burn per hour?

Answer:

QUESTION 14

You travel 700 NM. How much fuel will you need if you burn 80 lbs per hour, and are travelling at 500 kts?

Answer:

QUESTION 15

You travel at an average speed of 900 mph. How much fuel do you need for a 810 mile trip if you burn 60 kgs per hour?

Answer:

QUESTION 16

You have used 28 kgs of fuel in the past 1 hour and 52 mins. How much do you burn per hour?

Answer:

QUESTION 17

You travel at an average speed of 960 mph. How much fuel do you need for a 256 mile trip if you burn 150 kgs per hour?

Answer:

QUESTION 18

You travel 132 NM. How much fuel will you need if you burn 160 kgs per minute, and are travelling at 440 kts?

Answer:

QUESTION 19

You burn 42 kgs of fuel per hour. How much do you burn in 30 mins?

Answer:

QUESTION 20

You travel 11 miles. How much fuel will you need if you burn 21 kgs per minute, and are travelling at 33 mph?

Answer:

QUESTION 21

You burn 3 kgs of fuel per hour. How much do you burn in 40 mins?

Answer:

QUESTION 22

You travel 91 miles. How much fuel will you need if you burn 50 kgs per hour, and are travelling at 130 mph?

Answer:

QUESTION 23

You burn 48 kgs of fuel per hour. How much do you burn in 20 mins?

Answer:

QUESTION 24

You burn 12 kgs of fuel per hour. How much do you burn in 20 mins?

Answer:

QUESTION 25

You travel 205 NM. How much fuel will you need if you burn 180 kgs per hour, and are travelling at 820 kts?

Answer:

ANSWERS TO FUEL CALCULATION TEST 6

Question 1 – 9 kgs

Question 2 – 12 kgs

Question 3 – 75 kgs

Question 4 – 16 kgs

Question 5 – 720 kgs

Question 6 – 18 kgs

Question 7 – 22 kgs

Question 8 – 15 kgs

Question 9 – 140 kgs

Question 10 – 100 kgs

Question 11 – 4 lbs

Question 12 – 1 kg

Question 13 – 27 kgs

Question 14 – 112 lbs

Question 15 - 54 kgs

Question 16 – 15 kgs

Question 17 – 40 kgs

Question 18 – 2880 kgs

Question 19 - 21 kgs

Question 20 – 420 kgs

Question 21 – 2 kgs

Question 22 – 35 kgs

Question 23 – 16 kgs

Question 24 – 4 kgs

Question 25 – 45 kgs

FUEL CALCULATION TEST 7

QUESTION 1

You travel 288 NM. How much fuel will you need if you burn 24 kgs per hour, and are travelling at 432 kts?

Answer:

QUESTION 2

You burn 100 kgs of fuel per hour. How much fuel will you need to travel 850 miles if you average a speed of 1000 mph?

Answer:

QUESTION 3

You travel 27 miles. How much fuel will you need if you burn 72 kgs per hour, and are travelling at 324 mph?

Answer:

QUESTION 4

You travel 28 NM. How much fuel will you need if you burn 90 kgs per hour, and are travelling at 210 kts?

Answer:

QUESTION 5

You have used 100 kgs of fuel in the past 3 hours and 20 mins. How much do you burn per hour?

Answer:

QUESTION 6

You travel 360 miles. How much fuel will you need if you burn 160 kgs per hour, and are travelling at 900 mph?

Answer:

QUESTION 7

You burn 3 kgs of fuel per hour. How much do you burn in 40 mins?

Answer:

QUESTION 8

You travel 40 miles. How much fuel will you need if you burn 6 kgs per hour, and are travelling at 80 mph?

Answer:

QUESTION 9

You travel at an average speed of 585 mph. How much fuel do you need for a 234 mile trip if you burn 90 kgs per hour?

Answer:

QUESTION 10

You travel at an average speed of 148 mph. How much fuel do you need for a 37 mile trip if you burn 16 kgs per hour?

Answer:

QUESTION 11

You burn 60 kgs of fuel per hour. How much fuel will you need to travel 38 miles if you average a speed of 228 mph?

Answer:

QUESTION 12

You travel 9 miles. How much fuel will you need if you burn 45 kgs per hour, and are travelling at 45 mph?

Answer:

QUESTION 13

You burn 48 kgs of fuel per minute. How much do you burn in 1 hour?

Answer:

QUESTION 14

You travel 48 NM. How much fuel will you need if you burn 24 lbs per hour, and are travelling at 48 kts?

Answer:

QUESTION 15

You have used 66 kgs of fuel in the past 2 hours and 12 mins. How much do you burn per hour?

Answer:

QUESTION 16

You burn 30 kgs of fuel per minute. How much do you burn in 1 hour and 48 mins?

Answer:

QUESTION 17

You burn 12 kgs of fuel per hour. How much fuel will you need to travel 36 miles if you average a speed of 432 mph?

Answer:

QUESTION 18

You burn 90 kgs of fuel per minute. How much do you burn in 1 hour and 4 mins?

Answer:

QUESTION 19

You burn 15 kgs of fuel per hour. How much fuel will you need to travel 20 miles if you average a speed of 60 mph?

Answer:

QUESTION 20

You have used 84 kgs of fuel in the past 2 hours and 48 mins. How much do you burn per hour?

Answer:

QUESTION 21

You have used 416 kgs of fuel in the past 3 hours and 28 mins. How much do you burn per hour?

Answer:

QUESTION 22

You travel 9 NM. How much fuel will you need if you burn6 kgs per minute, and are travelling at 27 kts?

Answer:

QUESTION 23

You burn 25 kgs of fuel per hour. How much do you burn in 36 mins?

Answer:

QUESTION 24

You burn 20 kgs of fuel per minute. How much do you burn in 1 hour and 3 mins?

Answer:

QUESTION 25

You travel 700 miles. How much fuel will you need if you burn 120 kgs per minute, and are travelling at 840 mph?

Answer:

ANSWERS TO FUEL CALCULATION TEST 7

Question 1 – 16 kgs

Question 2 – 85 kgs

Question 3 – 6 kgs

Question 4 – 12 kgs

Question 5 – 30 kgs

Question 6 – 64 kgs

Question 7 – 2 kgs

Question 8 – 3 kgs

Question 9 – 36 kgs

Question 10 – 4 kgs

Question 11 – 10 kgs

Question 12 – 9 kgs

Question 13 – 2880 kgs

Question 14 – 24 lbs

Question 15 - 30 kgs

Question 16 – 3240 kgs

Question 17 – 1 kg

Question 18 – 5760 kgs

Question 19 - 5 kgs

Question 20 – 30 kgs

Question 21 – 120 kgs

Question 22 – 120 kgs

Question 23 – 15 kgs

Question 24 – 1260 kgs

Question 25 – 6000 kgs

FUEL CALCULATION TEST 8

QUESTION 1

You have used 776 kgs of fuel in the past 3 hours and 14 mins. How much do you burn per hour?

Answer:

QUESTION 2

You burn 15 kgs of fuel per hour. How much fuel will you need to travel 8 miles if you average a speed of 24 mph?

Answer:

QUESTION 3

You burn 30 kgs of fuel per hour. How much do you burn in 16 mins?

Answer:

QUESTION 4

You burn 135 kgs of fuel per hour. How much do you burn in 16 mins?

Answer:

QUESTION 5

You burn 9 kgs of fuel per hour. How much fuel will you need to travel 13 miles if you average a speed of 39 mph?

Answer:

QUESTION 6

You travel 138 NM. How much fuel will you need if you burn 30 kgs per hour, and are travelling at 230 kts?

Answer:

QUESTION 7

You burn 8 kgs of fuel per hour. How much do you burn in 30 mins?

Answer:

QUESTION 8

You have used 58 kgs of fuel in the past 2 hours and 25 mins. How much do you burn per hour?

Answer:

QUESTION 9

You burn 25 kgs of fuel per minute. How much do you burn in 12 mins?

Answer:

QUESTION 10

You travel at an average speed of 150 mph. How much fuel do you need for a 105 mile trip if you burn 90 kgs per hour?

Answer:

QUESTION 11

You burn 140 kgs of fuel per minute. How much do you burn in 33 mins?

Answer:

QUESTION 12

You have used 28 kgs of fuel in the past 3 hours and 30 mins. How much do you burn per hour?

Answer:

QUESTION 13

You burn 10 kgs of fuel per hour. How much do you burn in 12 mins?

Answer:

QUESTION 14

You travel 280 NM. How much fuel will you need if you burn 36 kgs per minute, and are travelling at 420 kts?

Answer:

QUESTION 15

You travel 26 miles. How much fuel will you need if you burn 24 kgs per hour, and are travelling at 312 mph?

Answer:

QUESTION 16

You travel 924 miles. How much fuel will you need if you burn 240 kgs per hour, and are travelling at 1320 mph?

Answer:

QUESTION 17

You burn 40 kgs of fuel per hour. How much do you burn in 42 mins?

Answer:

QUESTION 18

You have used 220 kgs of fuel in the past 1 hour and 28 mins. How much do you burn per hour?

Answer:

QUESTION 19

You burn 4 kgs of fuel per minute. How much do you burn in 1 hour and 30 mins?

Answer:

QUESTION 20

You burn 12 kgs of fuel per hour. How much do you burn in 30 mins?

Answer:

QUESTION 21

You travel 47 NM. How much fuel will you need if you burn 21 kgs per minute, and are travelling at 141 kts?

Answer:

QUESTION 22

You have used 63 kgs of fuel in the past 3 hours. How much do you burn per hour?

Answer:

QUESTION 23

You travel 986 NM. How much fuel will you need if you burn 240 kgs per hour, and are travelling at 1020 kts?

Answer:

QUESTION 24

You have used 123 kgs of fuel in the past 2 hours and 44 mins. How much do you burn per hour?

Answer:

QUESTION 25

You burn 21 kgs of fuel per minute. How much do you burn in 40 mins?

Answer:

ANSWERS TO FUEL CALCULATION TEST 8

Question 1 – 240 kgs

Question 2 – 5 kgs

Question 3 – 8 kgs

Question 4 – 36 kgs

Question 5 – 3 kgs

Question 6 – 18 kgs

Question 7 – 4 kgs

Question 8 – 24 kgs

Question 9 – 300 kgs

Question 10 – 63 kgs

Question 11 – 4620 kgs

Question 12 – 8 kgs

Question 13 – 2 kgs

Question 14 – 1440 kgs

Question 15 - 2 kgs

Question 16 – 168 kgs

Question 17 – 28 kgs

Question 18 – 150 kgs

Question 19 - 360 kgs

Question 20 – 6 kgs

Question 21 – 420 kgs

Question 22 – 21 kgs

Question 23 – 232 kgs

Question 24 – 45 kgs

Question 25 – 840 kgs

FUEL CALCULATION TEST 9

QUESTION 1

You burn 75 kgs of fuel per hour. How much fuel will you need to travel 200 miles if you average a speed of 375 mph?

Answer:

QUESTION 2

You have used 15 kgs of fuel in the past 1 hour and 15 mins. How much do you burn per hour?

Answer:

QUESTION 3

You travel 33 NM. How much fuel will you need if you burn 8 lbs per hour, and are travelling at 66 kts?

Answer:

QUESTION 4

You travel 333 miles. How much fuel will you need if you burn 30 kgs per hour, and are travelling at 185 mph?

Answer:

QUESTION 5

You burn 30 kgs of fuel per hour. How much fuel will you need to travel 88 miles if you average a speed of 132 mph?

Answer:

QUESTION 6

You travel 148 miles. How much fuel will you need if you burn 30 kgs per hour, and are travelling at 1110 mph?

Answer:

QUESTION 7

You travel 30 miles. How much fuel will you need if you burn 84 kgs per minute, and are travelling at 36 mph?

Answer:

QUESTION 8

You burn 90 kgs of fuel per hour. How much do you burn in 40 mins?

Answer:

QUESTION 9

You travel 342 NM. How much fuel will you need if you burn 90 kgs per minute, and are travelling at 570 kts?

Answer:

QUESTION 10

You have used 45 kgs of fuel in the past 3 hours and 45 mins. How much do you burn per hour?

Answer:

QUESTION 11

You burn 12 kgs of fuel per minute. How much do you burn in 5 mins?

Answer:

QUESTION 12

You travel 200 miles. How much fuel will you need if you burn 12 kgs per hour, and are travelling at 300 mph?

Answer:

QUESTION 13

You travel 9 NM. How much fuel will you need if you burn24 kgs per minute, and are travelling at 12 kts?

Answer:

QUESTION 14

You travel 12 NM. How much fuel will you need if you burn 50 kgs per hour, and are travelling at 30 kts?

Answer:

QUESTION 15

You burn 16 kgs of fuel per hour. How much fuel will you need to travel 11 miles if you average a speed of 22 mph?

Answer:

QUESTION 16

You burn 8 kgs of fuel per minute. How much do you burn in 1 hour and 30 mins?

Answer:

QUESTION 17

You burn 48 kgs of fuel per hour. How much fuel will you need to travel 156 miles if you average a speed of 234 mph?

Answer:

QUESTION 18

You burn 4 kgs of fuel per minute. How much do you burn in 1 hour?

Answer:

QUESTION 19

You travel 330 NM. How much fuel will you need if you burn 84 lbs per hour, and are travelling at 360 kts?

Answer:

QUESTION 20

You have used 117 kgs of fuel in the past 3 hours and 15 mins. How much do you burn per hour?

Answer:

QUESTION 21

You travel at an average speed of 410 mph. How much fuel do you need for a 205 mile trip if you burn 50 kgs per hour?

Answer:

QUESTION 22

You burn 14 kgs of fuel per hour. How much fuel will you need to travel 8 miles if you average a speed of 16 mph?

Answer:

QUESTION 23

You burn 84 kgs of fuel per minute. How much do you burn in 55 mins?

Answer:

QUESTION 24

You travel at an average speed of 184 mph. How much fuel do you need for a 46 mile trip if you burn 40 kgs per hour?

Answer:

QUESTION 25

You travel 225 NM. How much fuel will you need if you burn 42 kgs per hour, and are travelling at 270 kts?

Answer:

ANSWERS TO FUEL CALCULATION TEST 9

Question 1 – 40 kgs

Question 2 – 12 kgs

Question 3 – 4 lbs

Question 4 – 54 kgs

Question 5 – 20 kgs

Question 6 – 4 kgs

Question 7 – 4200 kgs

Question 8 – 60 kgs

Question 9 – 3240 kgs

Question 10 – 12 kgs

Question 11 – 60 kgs

Question 12 – 8 kgs

Question 13 – 1080 kgs

Question 14 – 20 kgs

Question 15 - 8 kgs

Question 16 – 720 kgs

Question 17 – 32 kgs

Question 18 – 240 kgs

Question 19 - 77 lbs

Question 20 – 36 kgs

Question 21 – 25 kgs

Question 22 – 7 kgs

Question 23 – 4620 kgs

Question 24 – 10 kgs

Question 25 – 35 kgs

FUEL CALCULATION TEST 10

QUESTION 1

You burn 12 kgs of fuel per minute. How much do you burn in 1 hour and 15 mins?

Answer:

QUESTION 2

You travel 304 NM. How much fuel will you need if you burn 210 kgs per hour, and are travelling at 570 kts?

Answer:

QUESTION 3

You travel 294 miles. How much fuel will you need if you burn 20 kgs per hour, and are travelling at 490 mph?

Answer:

QUESTION 4

You travel 98 NM. How much fuel will you need if you burn 40 kgs per minute, and are travelling at 245 kts?

Answer:

QUESTION 5

You have used 130 kgs of fuel in the past 1 hour and 18 mins. How much do you burn per hour?

Answer:

QUESTION 6

You have used 32 kgs of fuel in the past 2 hours. How much do you burn per hour?

Answer:

QUESTION 7

You travel 200 NM. How much fuel will you need if you burn 70 kgs per hour, and are travelling at 400 kts?

Answer:

QUESTION 8

You travel 80 miles. How much fuel will you need if you burn 20 kgs per minute, and are travelling at 160 mph?

Answer:

QUESTION 9

You travel 380 NM. How much fuel will you need if you burn 120 kgs per hour, and are travelling at 570 kts?

Answer:

QUESTION 10

You burn 60 kgs of fuel per hour. How much fuel will you need to travel 160 miles if you average a speed of 200 mph?

Answer:

QUESTION 11

You travel 228 NM. How much fuel will you need if you burn 12 lbs per hour, and are travelling at 152 kts?

Answer:

QUESTION 12

You burn 30 kgs of fuel per hour. How much do you burn in 50 mins?

Answer:

QUESTION 13

You have used 90 kgs of fuel in the past 2 hours. How much do you burn per hour?

Answer:

QUESTION 14

You have used 10 kgs of fuel in the past 50 mins. How much do you burn per hour?

Answer:

QUESTION 15

You travel at an average speed of 44 mph. How much fuel do you need for a 11 mile trip if you burn 36 kgs per hour?

Answer:

QUESTION 16

You have used 3 kgs of fuel in the past 30 mins. How much do you burn per hour?

Answer:

QUESTION 17

You burn 6 kgs of fuel per minute. How much do you burn in 1 hour and 40 mins?

Answer:

QUESTION 18

You burn 60 kgs of fuel per hour. How much do you burn in 44 mins?

Answer:

QUESTION 19

You burn 30 kgs of fuel per minute. How much do you burn in 1 hour?

Answer:

QUESTION 20

You travel 144 NM. How much fuel will you need if you burn 20 lbs per hour, and are travelling at 480 kts?

Answer:

QUESTION 21

You travel 105 miles. How much fuel will you need if you burn 5 kgs per hour, and are travelling at 175 mph?

Answer:

QUESTION 22

You burn 6 kgs of fuel per minute. How much do you burn in 1 hour?

Answer:

QUESTION 23

You burn 24 kgs of fuel per hour. How much do you burn in 15 mins?

Answer:

QUESTION 24

You burn 60 kgs of fuel per hour. How much do you burn in 45 mins?

Answer:

QUESTION 25

You travel 285 miles. How much fuel will you need if you burn 10 kgs per hour, and are travelling at 190 mph?

Answer:

ANSWERS TO FUEL CALCULATION TEST 10

Question 1 – 900 kgs

Question 2 – 112 kgs

Question 3 – 12 kgs

Question 4 – 960 kgs

Question 5 – 100 kgs

Question 6 – 16 kgs

Question 7 – 35 kgs

Question 8 – 600 kgs

Question 9 – 80 kgs

Question 10 – 48 kgs

Question 11 – 18 lbs

Question 12 – 25 kgs

Question 13 – 45 kgs

Question 14 – 12 kgs

Question 15 - 9 kgs

Question 16 – 6 kgs

Question 17 – 600 kgs

Question 18 – 44 kgs

Question 19 - 1800 kgs

Question 20 – 6 lbs

Question 21 – 3 kgs

Question 22 – 360 kgs

Question 23 – 6 kgs

Question 24 – 45 kgs

Question 25 – 15 kgs

FUEL CALCULATION TEST 11

QUESTION 1

You travel 330 NM. How much fuel will you need if you burn 200 lbs per hour, and are travelling at 300 kts?

Answer:

QUESTION 2

You have used 456 kgs of fuel in the past 3 hours and 48 mins. How much do you burn per hour?

Answer:

QUESTION 3

You have used 162 kgs of fuel in the past 3 hours and 36 mins. How much do you burn per hour?

Answer:

QUESTION 4

You travel at an average speed of 210 mph. How much fuel do you need for an 84 mile trip if you burn 25 kgs per hour?

Answer:

QUESTION 5

You burn 36 kgs of fuel per minute. How much do you burn in 10 mins?

Answer:

QUESTION 6

You travel 493 miles. How much fuel will you need if you burn 45 kgs per hour, and are travelling at 255 mph?

Answer:

QUESTION 7

You burn 28 kgs of fuel per minute. How much do you burn in 15 mins?

Answer:

QUESTION 8

You burn 90 kgs of fuel per minute. How much do you burn in 44 mins?

Answer:

QUESTION 9

You travel 100 NM. How much fuel will you need if you burn 24 kgs per minute, and are travelling at 200 kts?

Answer:

QUESTION 10

You travel 532 NM. How much fuel will you need if you burn 160 lbs per hour, and are travelling at 560 kts?

Answer:

QUESTION 11

You burn 90 kgs of fuel per minute. How much do you burn in 48 mins?

Answer:

QUESTION 12

You travel 74 miles. How much fuel will you need if you burn 20 kgs per minute, and are travelling at 185 mph?

Answer:

QUESTION 13

You have used 36 kgs of fuel in the past 3 hours. How much do you burn per hour?

Answer:

QUESTION 14

You burn 80 kgs of fuel per hour. How much fuel will you need to travel 42 miles if you average a speed of 70 mph?

Answer:

QUESTION 15

You burn 30 kgs of fuel per hour. How much do you burn in 30 mins?

Answer:

QUESTION 16

You travel 52 NM. How much fuel will you need if you burn 20 kgs per hour, and are travelling at 104 kts?

Answer:

QUESTION 17

You travel at an average speed of 48 mph. How much fuel do you need for a 4 mile trip if you burn 12 kgs per hour?

Answer:

QUESTION 18

You have used 56 kgs of fuel in the past 2 hours and 48 mins. How much do you burn per hour?

Answer:

QUESTION 19

You burn 48 kgs of fuel per minute. How much do you burn in 30 mins?

Answer:

QUESTION 20

You travel 1518 miles. How much fuel will you need if you burn 150 kgs per hour, and are travelling at 1380 mph?

Answer:

QUESTION 21

You burn 160 kgs of fuel per minute. How much do you burn in 15 mins?

Answer:

QUESTION 22

You travel 39 NM. How much fuel will you need if you burn 2 kgs per minute, and are travelling at 78 kts?

Answer:

QUESTION 23

You have used 10 kgs of fuel in the past 24 mins. How much do you burn per hour?

Answer:

QUESTION 24

You travel at an average speed of 14 mph. How much fuel do you need for a 7 mile trip if you burn 10 kgs per hour?

Answer:

QUESTION 25

You burn 36 kgs of fuel per minute. How much do you burn in 40 mins?

Answer:

ANSWERS TO FUEL CALCULATION TEST 11

Question 1 - 220 lbs

Question 2 – 120 kgs

Question 3 – 45 kgs

Question 4 – 10 kgs

Question 5 – 360 kgs

Question 6 – 87 kgs

Question 7 – 420 kgs

Question 8 – 3960 kgs

Question 9 – 720 kgs

Question 10 – 152 lbs

Question 11 – 4320 kgs

Question 12 – 480 kgs

Question 13 – 12 kgs

Question 14 – 48 kgs

Question 15 - 15 kgs

Question 16 – 10 kgs

Question 17 – 1 kg

Question 18 – 20 kgs

Question 19 - 1440 kgs

Question 20 – 165 kgs

Question 21 – 2400 kgs

Question 22 – 60 kgs

Question 23 – 25 kgs

Question 24 – 5 kgs

Question 25 – 1440 kgs

FUEL CALCULATION TEST 12

QUESTION 1

You burn 100 kgs of fuel per hour. How much fuel will you need to travel 12 miles if you average a speed of 30 mph?

Answer:

QUESTION 2

You travel at an average speed of 68 mph. How much fuel do you need for a 34 mile trip if you burn 16 kgs per hour?

Answer:

QUESTION 3

You have used 70 kgs of fuel in the past 1 hour and 24 mins. How much do you burn per hour?

Answer:

QUESTION 4

You burn 35 kgs of fuel per hour. How much do you burn in 12 mins?

Answer:

QUESTION 5

You travel 1350 NM. How much fuel will you need if you burn 30 lbs per hour, and are travelling at 810 kts?

Answer:

QUESTION 6

You travel 19 miles. How much fuel will you need if you burn 14 kgs per minute, and are travelling at 38 mph?

Answer:

QUESTION 7

You burn 70 kgs of fuel per minute. How much do you burn in 54 mins?

Answer:

QUESTION 8

You travel 6 miles. How much fuel will you need if you burn 10 kgs per hour, and are travelling at 4 mph?

Answer:

QUESTION 9

You burn 60 kgs of fuel per hour. How much fuel will you need to travel 408 miles if you average a speed of 480 mph?

Answer:

QUESTION 10

You travel 6 NM. How much fuel will you need if you burn70 kgs per hour, and are travelling at 10 kts?

Answer:

QUESTION 11

You travel 42 miles. How much fuel will you need if you burn 21 kgs per minute, and are travelling at 126 mph?

Answer:

QUESTION 12

You travel 585 NM. How much fuel will you need if you burn 210 lbs per hour, and are travelling at 1350 kts?

Answer:

QUESTION 13

You travel at an average speed of 720 mph. How much fuel do you need for a 312 mile trip if you burn 150 kgs per hour?

Answer:

QUESTION 14

You burn 60 kgs of fuel per hour. How much fuel will you need to travel 506 miles if you average a speed of 552 mph?

Answer:

QUESTION 15

You travel 123 miles. How much fuel will you need if you burn 10 kgs per minute, and are travelling at 205 mph?

Answer:

QUESTION 16

You travel 20 NM. How much fuel will you need if you burn 90 kgs per minute, and are travelling at 600 kts?

Answer:

QUESTION 17

You travel 136 miles. How much fuel will you need if you burn 80 kgs per hour, and are travelling at 340 mph?

Answer:

QUESTION 18

You burn 16 kgs of fuel per hour. How much do you burn in 45 mins?

Answer:

QUESTION 19

You travel 144 NM. How much fuel will you need if you burn 140 kgs per hour, and are travelling at 480 kts?

Answer:

QUESTION 20

You burn 84 kgs of fuel per hour. How much do you burn in 10 mins?

Answer:

QUESTION 21

You travel 192 miles. How much fuel will you need if you burn 60 kgs per hour, and are travelling at 480 mph?

Answer:

QUESTION 22

You travel 18 miles. How much fuel will you need if you burn 5 kgs per hour, and are travelling at 30 mph?

Answer:

QUESTION 23

You burn 12 kgs of fuel per minute. How much do you burn in 40 mins?

Answer:

QUESTION 24

You burn 48 kgs of fuel per hour. How much fuel will you need to travel 120 miles if you average a speed of 240 mph?

Answer:

QUESTION 25

You burn 42 kgs of fuel per minute. How much do you burn in 1 hour and 10 mins?

Answer:

ANSWERS TO FUEL CALCULATION TEST 12

Question 1 - 40 kgs

Question 2 – 8 kgs

Question 3 – 50 kgs

Question 4 – 7 kgs

Question 5 – 50 lbs

Question 6 – 420 kgs

Question 7 – 3780 kgs

Question 8 – 15 kgs

Question 9 – 51 kgs

Question 10 – 42 kgs

Question 11 – 420 kgs

Question 12 – 91 lbs

Question 13 - 65 kgs

Question 14 – 55 kgs

Question 15 - 360 kgs

Question 16 – 180 kgs

Question 17 – 32 kgs

Question 18 – 12 kgs

Question 19 - 42 kgs

Question 20 – 14 kgs

Question 21 – 24 kgs

Question 22 – 3 kgs

Question 23 – 480 kgs

Question 24 – 24 kgs

Question 25 – 2940 kgs

A FEW FINAL WORDS

Congratulations on reaching the end of the workbook. Before I sign off, I want to provide you with some details about what your results mean and how an employer will use them to assess you for the position you are applying for.

WHAT IS A GOOD SCORE?

It is difficult to pinpoint what exactly is a good score. The reason for this is because the majority of employers will use your scores in the fuel calculation test in **conjunction** with your scores from any other element of assessment/testing you are required to undertake as part of the selection process. You may even find that the requirement to answer fuel calculation tests forms part of another exercise or assessment, such as a planning exercise or group discussion.

The assessor/employer will usually also compare your test marks against those who have previously sat the test. This is often referred to as a **comparison group**. It is now more common for an assessor to grade your scores in the test compared to the previous comparison group, as opposed to giving you a definitive score. For example, you could be graded as follows:

- Your scores are well above average compared to previous test takers in this category.
- Your scores are above average compared to previous test takers in this category.

- Your scores are in the average range for those who have previously sat this test.
- Your scores are below average compared to previous test takers in this category.

I am sorry that I cannot provide you with any further information that relates to the scoring system used during this type of assessment but it is important to aim for both speed and accuracy. I also strongly recommend that you attempt to answer these questions without the use of a calculator.

Finally, as a gesture of goodwill and to further help you prepare, if you go to the following website I will provide you with free access to online psychometric tests:

WWW.PSYCHOMETRICTESTSONLINE.CO.UK

Good luck in your tests.

Kind regards

Richard McMunn